It's Okay

...to be a Mum

Torn Curtain Publishing
Wellington, New Zealand
www.torncurtainpublishing.com

© Copyright 2022 Leitu Kimitaunga. All rights reserved.

ISBN Softcover 978-0-473-63468-1

No portion of this book may be reproduced, stored in a retrieval system or transmitted in any form or by any means—electronic, mechanical, photocopy, recording or otherwise—except for brief quotations in printed reviews or promotion, without prior written permission from the author.

Some names and identifying details of people described in this book have been altered to protect their privacy.

Unless otherwise noted, all scripture is taken from the Holy Bible, New International Version®, NIV®. Copyright © 1973, 1978, 1984, 2011 by Biblica, Inc.™ Used by permission of Zondervan. All rights reserved worldwide.

Scripture quotations marked NLT are taken from the Holy Bible, New Living Translation, copyright © 1996, 2004, 2015 by Tyndale House Foundation. Used by permission of Tyndale House Publishers, Inc., Carol Stream, Illinois 60188. All rights reserved.

Scriptures marked NKJV are taken from the New King James Version®. Copyright © 1982 by Thomas Nelson. Used by permission. All rights reserved.

Cover art by Tara Zahn. Used with permission.

Cataloguing in Publishing Data
Title: It's Okay to be a Mum
Author: Leitu Kimitaunga
Subjects: Personal memoir, Christian life, Women's issues, Family and parenting, Spiritual growth
Typeset in Palatino Linotype, Merienda and Poppins.

A copy of this title is held at the National Library of New Zealand.

It's Okay

...to be a Mum

Leitu Kimitaunga

To my Mum

*I'm able to be a great mother because you first taught me how—
by simply being a mother yourself.*

Thank you, Mum!

Contents

Introduction 1
1   Upbringing 5
2   "Run!" 9
3   Tangled in Sin 13
4   Losing my Way 17
5   Untrue Love 19
6   Coming Home 23
7   Addicted 26
8   A New Start 29
9   Giving Up Control 32
10   Dying to Self 35
11   Who's the Breadwinner? 38
12   Identity 42
13   Discover your Beauty 46
14   The Power of Porn 50
15   Dealing with Insecurity 54
16   Our Genealogy 57

17	Overcoming Loneliness	60
18	A Father's Love	64
19	A Change of Attitude	68
20	Loving Difficult People	71
21	Forgiveness	75
22	Solo Parenting	78
23	Enjoying Motherhood	82
24	Life with Christ	85
25	The Enemy	88
26	No Excuses	92
	In closing	96

Introduction

If you like honesty, openness and truth given in a raw, un-sugar-coated way, this is the book for you! It is the story of my life, from my childhood growing up in the church, to my teenage years, to being a young mother dealing with addiction and an abusive relationship, and then ending right back where I started—in church, but this time completely transformed.

I have seen God do things that only He can. I've seen Him move in unexpected ways. I can testify that He cares for each and every one of us! Each of us has an important purpose and a unique life story. What follows is a small snippet of mine.

As a woman, I've always had hopes and dreams. But when I became a mum, I had to figure out my purpose all over again. I know I'm not alone in this. The world places intense pressure on young mums, and a lot of this comes from social media. Sometimes it seems no matter what you do (or don't do!) it's never good enough.

Are you sick and tired of doing things in your own strength, in your own way, and failing? Does it feel like you are just doing, always doing, and more doing? Are you running on empty, tired and worn out? Well, I was! But God showed me another way, a way not marked by failure but full of courageous action, self-love, and happiness. That's how I became stronger and discovered my worth as a mother, a partner, and a daughter of the Highest—by doing things God's way. And guess what? So can you!

The very first step is surrender—giving up our preconceived ideas of what life should be like, what it means to be a woman, and a mother. I had to decide that instead of letting this world dictate who I should be, I would base my identity on God's Word. When I did that, although it didn't happen overnight like we all wish it would, life got easier. I started to see things differently. God showed me I had to be one hundred percent honest about who I was, trusting that what He revealed wasn't designed to hurt me or make me feel ashamed, but to make me aware of the burdens I carried. I had to get rid of all the internal junk I was hauling around. It was time to be set free!

I believe this book will help anyone who reads it with an open heart and mind. I still have baggage, and my problems haven't disappeared instantly, but my story contains hope. I'm still in the process of becoming all I was created to be, but I'm not doing it alone. Still, as you read my story, you may feel offended by some of what I say. That's okay. My intention in sharing my story is not to cast blame or hurt anyone, but to help you dig a little deeper and find significance in what God has called you to do. In my own life, I have found that offence is usually triggered by an issue within my heart that needs dealing with. If you feel offended at any point, I encourage you to ask yourself *why* you feel that way. I urge you to stop what you're doing, calm your emotions, and begin to process. If you don't know where to start, pray. God will help you and show you what to do. He truly has all the answers!

It is my hope that this book will bring freedom, or at least some sort

INTRODUCTION

of relief, to women who are struggling with their responsibilities and situations—from singleness to motherhood, from addiction to promiscuity. You are not alone! I've experienced difficulties that some of you may be able to relate to. Or maybe you've got your own set of struggles. Wherever you're at, I want you to know that it's okay to be 'just' a mother, to not be out at work all day, or to not be organised at home! It's okay to have bad mornings and rough days. It's okay to cry or feel overwhelmed. It's okay! Whatever is going on in your life, I want you to know you're going to be okay! I can say that with confidence because I believe that what God did for me, He will do for you also.

1

Upbringing

Start children off on the way they should go, and even when they are old they will not turn from it.

Proverbs 22:6

My mother was a solo parent, but she raised me and my siblings in the church. Going to church was a highlight of my week. I looked forward to hanging out with other kids in Sunday School, enjoying biscuits and cordial afterwards, and finding familiar faces in the crowd. After church, Mum would stop at the local bakery to get fresh bread which we'd enjoy with the roast dinner she'd have prepared earlier. It's an after-church tradition I continue with my own children—with the occasional takeaway meal thrown in every now and then!

Being a mother myself, I now understand why my mum relied on our church family for support. With the responsibilities and pressures of being a parent, she knew that raising us in the church was the best thing she could do for us. We attended every Sunday. To this day I love my mother for setting that foundation for us as kids. Even so, I never fully understood why we went to church or who God was. I knew all the stories in the Bible and I could say the Lord's Prayer. I knew what Jesus had done for me on the cross, that He had paid the penalty for my sin, and that He wanted to be my Saviour. But as a child, I never had a personal relationship with Him.

As I grew into my teenage years, going to church became something I just did, even if my heart wasn't in it. I still believe there is no safer place for a teenager to be on a Friday night than at a church youth group, but when you turn up simply because your parents want you to be there, it's easy to end up focused on the social scene, not on God. I was a younger teen hanging out with older girls who were there for the wrong reasons, and it rubbed off on me. I was still trying to figure out who I was, and I was easily influenced.

Before long my church attendance revolved around boys and the hip-hop dance group. Because I had never had my own encounter with Jesus, I felt out of place. I had no idea what the church leaders were talking about when they spoke of experiencing His love or presence. Still, my sister and I looked like good, well-behaved Christian teenagers. Dance was our thing and we were really good at it. We even performed on stage with the dance group. But ultimately it wasn't enough to keep us there. By my mid-teens, my attitude, the way I saw myself, and how I viewed life, had already changed.

Being a Christian at high school was never popular or easy. I felt like I was the only one in the entire school who attended church. I hated sticking out. I was ashamed to tell people about my faith so I hid that side of me, keeping it a big secret. I put on masks and performances for people because I was unhappy with who I was. I let the opinions of others have power over me; this was the motivation behind my actions and the decisions I made. I always wanted praise from people, and pleasing them was very important to me when it shouldn't have been. I was torn between two worlds; the secret life as a believer and the other, trying to fit in with society.

When our family moved from one side of Auckland to the other, we had a discussion about church and realised it wasn't the same anymore. We were no longer little children; we were teens, and we didn't enjoy attending. My mother left the decision of whether or not we kept going up to us.

This was a huge change! I was only sixteen when my sister and I decided not to continue going to church. Away from church's influence, we started to live lives coloured by the world. I began doing a lot of things behind my mother's back. That was the beginning of many years of sinful living apart from God.

As a mother, it scares me now to think of my own children going through that same thing. I wonder if my mother felt that sort of fear. I have to keep reminding myself to trust God with my children's futures. He is a loving Father and will take care of them. This is why I personally love Proverbs 22:6. It gives me the assurance that even if my children decide to explore life without God, they will always have Jesus to turn to.

That's how it was for me. Although I had never understood having a personal relationship with God or experienced it for myself, the foundations had been laid. No matter what I did or what I went through in the years that followed, He was there, somewhere, listening, and watching me. He was always my first point of contact when I needed help. I ran to Him and He always answered. Still, it took a dramatic situation for God to get my attention and ultimately lead me back to Him.

2

"Run!"

I will certainly keep you safe from these wicked men.
I will rescue you from their cruel hands.

Jeremiah 15:21, NLT

When I was a little girl, around the age of six, I was told by my mother that I was not allowed to go to my friend's house and play. I remember that discussion vividly, like it was yesterday. While my mother was busy, I opened the front door and left to go exactly where I'd been forbidden.

As much as I try to remember my friend's name, it never comes to me even though this little friend often came over to my house to play and hang out. For some reason, my mind has chosen to forget. If I close my eyes and think about her, I remember she never wore shoes and her hair was never brushed, it was always tangled and messy. Her clothes had holes in them, and she often had bruises on her arms. I never thought anything of this until she reappeared in my memories as an adult. Whenever I think about her, I start crying, because I now see that what I went through is nothing compared to what she must have endured.

Do you want to know something really weird? I had never been to my friend's house before the day my mother gave me that warning, and I can't even remember how I knew where she lived. When I arrived at her house, she answered the door and her reaction said it all. She quietly asked, "What are you doing here?"

Her stepfather came to the door and told me to come in and play. Excited, I went inside. We went into the lounge. It was small, and I thought it was odd: There was a bed in the living area, right opposite the dining table and chairs. My friend sat there quietly with her head down and her stepfather offered me some water, which I drank, and that's all I remember. I know now he had spiked my drink and I was knocked out. I don't know what happened, or how I woke up. At some point, it was like something just switched on and I was instantly awake.

As I sat up, I realised that I was on that bed in the lounge and that my pants and underwear were around my ankles. Without hesitation I pulled them up, rubbed my eyes, and looked around the room. The lounge was filled with strange men. I started to freak out, and then I heard a voice, a loud whisper in my ear: "Run!"

I honestly don't know how I made it out the door. As I started running, I heard my friend yelling at me to slow down, begging me to come back and not tell anyone. I remember telling her she wasn't my friend anymore, then I turned around and bolted for home. As soon as I got to my house, my mind went blank. My mother asked me where I had been. Everyone had been looking for me. I told her I was at my friend's house and that I fell asleep. At just six years old, I couldn't understand what had happened to me.

Looking back, I believe my brain went straight into protection mode. As a result, I grew up quite happily. I was largely unaffected by that incident, and I never played the victim. The trauma of what took place was buried in my brain for many, many years until God revealed it to me in a series of dreams. In fact, they were worse than dreams, more like nightmares, and I suffered them every day for a whole week.

I knew what I was seeing in those dreams was real because they perfectly matched the broken memories I had been trying to piece together. I now understood what had happened to me. Even so, for a long time I didn't want to share it with anyone because I wasn't sure if they would believe me. This was the hardest thing I'd ever had to share, and I carried it for years. I was ashamed to tell anyone. I don't know why I was ashamed; I just was. The enemy, Satan, kept whispering in my ear that what happened that day was my fault, that I could never get my life back again, and I believed him.

I am so thankful for God's restoration. Without Him, I wouldn't be able to share this story or tell you how powerful and amazing God's love is. After He showed me what happened, I began to experience healing and found the strength I needed to share it with my mother, my sisters, and my partner. I don't know why I had been so worried. When I talked about it with my mother, she remembered asking me why I had blood on my underwear. She thought it was odd, and had gone looking for me, but was unable to find me.

I never saw my friend again. After that day, she never came back to school or came over to play. I hope one day I will see her again.

But mostly, I am thankful to God, who urged me to run from that house, took the trauma from me to protect me from more harm, then resurfaced the memory only when I was able to handle it. And I am so thankful for my mother's prayers. I believe her prayers kept me psychologically healthy as a child, despite what I went through. God's Word is true.

When we lay a foundation of faith for our children, we can be sure they will one day return to God and encounter His love, however tough their journey may be. Romans 8:28 says, "And we know that in all things God works for the good of those who love him, who have been called according to his purpose."

3

Tangled in Sin

Neither height nor depth, nor anything else in all creation, will be able to separate us from the love of God that is in Christ Jesus our Lord.

Romans 8:39

What is addiction? Put simply, it is an ongoing urge to do something that is hard to control or stop. This comes in many forms, and I experienced this in my own life through drug addiction. I was addicted to smoking marijuana. It's not as big a problem as meth, also known as 'P', but it ruled my life. For a long time, I used it every day.

It started when I was in intermediate school, somewhere between twelve and thirteen years old. I had seen older family members smoke marijuana and I wanted to see what all the fuss was about. Let's just say, I liked it, a lot! It made me feel happy. Afterwards, I had the 'mean munchies'. When I smoked weed, I had a limitless appetite and ate whatever was in sight. What more could a pre-teen want?

My drug habit started out innocently enough, but I got a taste for marijuana right away and it was easy to get into my hands. I could even get it for free. When I was in high school, the crowd I hung out with also smoked marijuana. We smoked before school, during lunch breaks, and after school. We would be so high our eyes were bloodshot. As a young teen, I found that feeling to be pure awesomeness.

I didn't come from a typical broken home, but my father was mostly absent. My dad was unfaithful to my mum, and when I was still little they separated. My dad had another wife and family, and although he turned up every now and then, his visits were out of the blue, and always very short. As a result, I never really knew my dad, and I'm sure he had no idea what was going on in my life.

By the time I reached my teenage years, my mother was exhausted, worn down by life. My mum allowed me to do whatever I wanted because she trusted me, and I did my best to make her believe I was doing nothing inappropriate. Looking back now, I suspect she knew the truth of the matter. There were times when she asked me if I was stoned, and I would make excuses. So much nonsense came out of my mouth, but she never gave me a lecture or a growling. She was always mellow with me.

As exciting as that freedom was at the time, it made me vulnerable as I ended up in situations that I shouldn't have been in. Looking back, I'm thankful I was never alone; I always had my girlfriends from school with me. We did things together and somehow, we managed to stay safe. I made many stupid decisions like lying about where I was staying and what I was doing just for a good night and not wanting to miss out. I knew for a fact that if I told my mother I wanted to go out drinking, I would get a big fat no and maybe even a slap.

I did a lot of things that I didn't want to do because I was trying to fit in. I smoked cigarettes, skipped classes, and wagged school. I lost my virginity because everyone my age was doing it, and if you hadn't 'done it', they mocked you and decided you weren't 'cool'. I was following the crowd, and partly this was because I struggled with my ethnicity. I'm part Māori and part Samoan, and I found it hard to fit in with either group. I had friends who were Samoan. They knew their culture and spoke the language fluently, whereas I only knew four words in Samoan. I felt more comfortable with my Māori friends as I grew up surrounded by my Māori cousins, but I still found myself putting on masks when I was around them.

I acted differently around different people. It didn't matter if I was with a certain ethnic group, or my family, or the churchy bunch–I wasn't myself. I layered lies on top of more lies until I realised that they were starting to catch up with me. Hiding who I was became a habit, a habit which was hard to keep up. The more I lied, the more people took advantage of me. I allowed this to happen because I refused to say no and be honest.

It came to a head when some 'friends' asked me to carry cannabis and alcohol to a party for them because they didn't want to get caught. I'm guessing, just like me, they didn't want their parents to find out either. I agreed, even though I did not want to. At the party, however, one of my friends got drunk to the point of being wasted. Someone called the police, and an ambulance came to take her to the hospital where she was diagnosed with alcohol poisoning. When she was questioned, she blamed me and told the police that I was the one who had brought the alcohol to the party.

I remember thanking God that I hadn't been drinking that night—in fact, my best friend and I were leaving the party sober just as the police arrived. I was glad I'd chosen not to get drunk or 'high' at the party. But for the first time I realised that I could've been the one who landed in serious trouble. After that, I decided to be completely honest with those around me. It wasn't worth the trouble that came with faking it, telling lies, or trying to be someone I wasn't.

Now as I look back on my younger days, childless and free to do whatever I wanted, without responsibilities, I am thankful that time is just a memory. I had no sense of direction or what I wanted for myself in the future. I had nothing to work towards. I just wanted to enjoy life, but I was all over the place, a complete mess. The reason I looked forward to the weekends was only for the late-night partying, and getting drunk and stoned. Waking up the next morning with a hangover and a thumping headache wasn't exactly cool, but I didn't think much about that. I just didn't want others to know. I had learnt how to hide. I was living a double life.

4

Losing my Way

If you do not do what is right, sin is crouching at your door;
it desires to have you, but you must rule over it.

Genesis 4:7

I spent my teenage years trying to please other people. I would give things away, laugh at stupid jokes and tell people things they wanted to hear, even if I didn't want to say it. More than anything else, I wanted the approval of others. I valued what they thought and said about me above what God thinks about me. I didn't think much of it at first, but small lies always led to bigger lies. Soon I was lying to people and to myself, and it led me into sin. I hated the taste and smell of cigarettes, but I ended up smoking them. I consumed alcohol and drugs, all because my friends were. I wanted to be cool, to be 'good enough'.

At the age of seventeen, I decided to leave school. I was wagging every class except Physical Education, so there was no point in me attending school anyway. I decided to enrol myself in a course to study fitness and sports. I gained a qualification as a lifeguard, which I used to get a job at a local pool. This was the first time ever I had felt like an adult. Suddenly I could buy things and help my mother out if she needed something. It was great! At the same time, I felt lost. I had no idea what I was supposed to do next.

I quickly got bored of going to work, coming home, and doing nothing. My eldest sister was living away from home. My other sister, who I had always hung out with, was still at home, but she was nineteen and already had two children, so she was busy tending to them. My younger brother was still a pre-teen. I didn't want to hang out with him. I was a 'responsible adult', and that meant toning down the drinking and partying. In any case, once I was legally old enough to purchase alcohol, the excitement and hype from sneaking out and getting wasted wasn't even cool anymore. I was a young woman, but I felt old. My friends were all busy with their own lives, and I soon became lonely.

Having no sense of direction is very dangerous. You start looking for things to do which may seem like great ideas, but really, they are not! I was seeking attention and ended up finding it by sleeping around. At first, I liked it, but even that soon changed. I was still seventeen when I found out I was pregnant.

5

Untrue Love

The way of fools seems right to them, but the wise listen to advice.

Proverbs 12:15

I first met Marc when I was still at school. He was older than me by a few years, and I thought he was charming. We soon exchanged numbers and started messaging each other. Then we began dating. Everyone liked Marc—except for my dad. I remember him coming over one day when Marc was at our house. After he met him, my dad took me to another room and tried to have a heart-to-heart with me. "I know guys like that," he warned me. "Be careful. They're only after one thing."

At the time, I didn't listen. I let anger get in the way. Why did my dad suddenly care who I dated? I couldn't believe he'd been absent all those years, and now he wanted to have *this* conversation. In retrospect, I wish I'd listened to my dad. Instead, I decided to move in with my new boyfriend. What can I say? I was so blinded by what I thought love was that I couldn't see the problems in the early stages of our relationship. It started off awesome . . . you know, the 'honeymoon' stage. But that quickly disappeared and suddenly, life got real when I found out I was pregnant.

There was no sense of excitement when I found out we were going to have a baby. Marc had no job, and already his initial charm had started to wear off. All I knew was that he wanted me to use my 'benefit' money to buy marijuana, that he had no interest in getting a job, and that he was out of the house a lot. When I asked him about where he'd been, he denied sleeping around, even though it was obvious. I soon realised I had no idea who this guy was that I had ended up with.

We went along with the pregnancy, but when I was thirty-six weeks pregnant, I found out that my partner was still cheating on me, and it was desperately painful. This was the first time in my life I became depressed. It was a horrible feeling. And yet I thought I loved him.

When our baby girl was born, we called her Sophia. From the moment I saw her, I loved her with an indescribable love. I had given up smoking weed while I was pregnant, but soon after her birth, I started smoking again. Weed was always around, and it only led to more problems. Marc often asked me to buy weed out of my sole parent benefit, and most of the time, I agreed. But if I pushed back at all or stood my ground, we'd usually end up in an argument, which sometimes turned violent. That began a cycle of me leaving him, then taking him back. I really felt like I loved him—I just wished he could get a job rather than lean on me for support. But I was also desperate for attention. It's no excuse for what he eventually did, but at the time, I put so much pressure on him to make me happy. I was such a little girl! I had no idea about my own worth, and I was confused.

I fell pregnant not once but twice to this same man. Obviously, I did not learn! I missed all the signs. A little more than a year later we found out another baby was on its way.

When our second daughter was born, we named her Phyllis, after my mother. She too was a delight, but life at home became increasingly difficult. Now that we had two kids, I wanted Marc to earn some money and take responsibility. It felt like he was all talk and not enough action, but whenever I brought up the subject of work, he got mad.

Gradually Marc became more violent. It began with him slapping me around, and then I'd tell him to leave. Then I'd think about how much I missed him and loved him, and I'd ask him to come home. But the more I took him back, the more he slapped me around. It didn't help that I was the type of person that if anyone hit me, I was going to hit back. No way would I back down from a fight. I had a big mouth, and I thought I was so tough!

I'm sure many women can relate. So often we expect our significant other to make us happy, as if it's their responsibility (really, it isn't!). But however unrealistic our expectations are, it does not excuse anyone for laying their hands on anyone else. By now, whenever Marc was in a rage, I became his punching bag. He'd hit me and drag me around the house until I was bruised all over.

A few years later, Marc still couldn't seem to get work in New Zealand, so when his father, who lived in Australia, offered him a job working for him, we made the decision to leave New Zealand.

We moved over to Australia and things were supposed to get better, but they didn't. My father had also moved his family over there by that time, and initially we lived with him. That only lasted until he spoke some harsh words to Marc and I stuck up for him. I know . . . what an idiot! I may have never been close to my father, but I knew he was only looking out for me. Anyway, being stupid, we moved in with another relative who we did not know. I must say, he was a very nice man! I'm truly grateful he opened up his home to us.

Still, we were in a foreign country and had no idea what the hell we were doing. Marc only lasted a week in the job we had gone over there for. Now neither of us were working. I was not happy and I felt sorry for my girls. I got some government assistance, but it wasn't much, and there was no sign things were going to get better. In fact, Marc became even more abusive, to the point where I tried to leave him for good. Marc did not like that one bit. That day, he locked me in a room and gave me the biggest hiding ever! He threatened me and told me if I ever left again, the next beating would be even worse. Thank God that his uncle returned home from work just at the right time. Even so, I was terrified for my life.

I decided to return to New Zealand and my family helped me get a flight. In the end, Marc came back with me, but I planned to leave him as soon as we landed. When I arrived at Auckland airport and people asked about the bruising on my face, I lied about it. I felt ashamed and didn't want to reveal how 'weak' I had been to let a man hit me. Even so, I couldn't get away. My partner knew I was trying to leave, and he hung around close, like a bad smell.

6

Coming Home

*He led me to a place of safety; he rescued
me because he delights in me.*

Psalm 18:19, NLT

Back in New Zealand, life got even worse. I had been broken down physically, mentally, and spiritually. The woman I once was had been beaten so badly I viewed myself as scared, worthless, useless, and pathetic. All I knew was, I clearly needed saving! And so, I decided to go back to church with my mum.

Soon after, I had the same dream every day for a whole week, only, it felt like a nightmare. It was so frustrating! In the dream, everywhere I went and no matter what I did, this tiny, weeny frog was with me. Attached to this frog was a string. No matter what I did to try and break the string, that stupid, annoying little frog would always be around or would reappear. It was like shooing away a fly, only it keeps coming back. Well, if you guessed that the frog represented Marc, you're absolutely right! I didn't realise at the time it was God warning me.

When a church friend interpreted this dream, I was gobsmacked because I knew it to be true in my heart. Even though I had tried to leave Marc multiple times, it never worked. He showed he had changed (so I thought), I was sucked in, and everything went back to normal, but it never lasted. It was a continuous cycle that was on repeat for years. I had no confidence in myself, I was still scared of him, and I let fear control me. For years, I'd asked him over and over to leave, but he refused. Instead, he would lock me and the girls in the house so I couldn't run away, and take my phone so I couldn't ring the police or my family. He would take my car keys and hide them. I even had to go to the toilet with the door open, and at times he kept me isolated from the girls.

Then one day, just as I was literally being choked to death, I found the will to fight. Marc's hands were squeezed around my throat, and I was ready to die. And in that moment, I heard a voice say, "You're going to leave your girls with him." I don't know what happened next but I managed to get myself out of his chokehold and started fighting back. Something switched and I had fight in me once again. My partner was furious and threatened to take the kids away from me—the same old tirade. Barricading myself and the girls in my room, I remember falling to my knees to bawl my eyes out, begging God to help me, to send someone over or provide some form of escape.

I was completely drained from keeping up appearances, putting on masks and performing like we were so in love and our family was so perfect! I couldn't allow my children to think it was okay, that this was how couples acted and treated each other, that this is what love looked like. No way! I couldn't do it anymore! It was time for me to step up and be the mother I knew I was all along.

I know God heard me—my sister came over and Marc was gone. He must have run away. This was God giving me the opportunity to sort my life out. I went to my mum's place and rang the police. They did a house check to make sure he wasn't in my house and issued a trespass order. Thankfully, that was all it took. I had stayed with him for nine years—now I did what was necessary for us to live safely and happily.

That wasn't the end of things. I went to stay with my mum, but like in my dream, he hung around, stalking me on social media, messaging me, contacting my family and friends to find out what I was doing or if I was going anywhere. He was that annoying little frog that wouldn't go away. He was persistent and took drastic actions to force his way back into my world, but I knew God had other plans for me. All I can say is that if I can get out, so can you! You are valuable and worth so much. God hears you and sees you every day, you just have to take that first step.

7

Addicted

He has sent me to proclaim freedom for the prisoners and recovery of sight for the blind, to set the oppressed free.

Luke 4:18

In Australia I had tried to break my addiction to weed. Basically, the habit had become too expensive, especially for someone who didn't earn very much. When I first met Marc, he was already addicted to it, but at the time I couldn't see it. I didn't even know what addiction was until I started to notice the ugly side of this person I had 'fallen in love with'. Marijuana was all he thought about. Smoking it was the first thing he did in the morning, and the last thing he did at night. But he wasn't the one who was buying it, that was me. If I said no or didn't hand money over, he would throw a tantrum and get violent. That kind of behaviour was common, but he considered it to be normal and

I played my part too, giving him the money when he wanted it.

As I look back, I tried so many times to stop my own marijuana habit but I had a fear of missing out and I reasoned that if I was paying for it then why shouldn't I have my fun too? So, there I was again and again, sharing joints with him and some family members. Everyone seemed so happy, talking nonsense and acting like we were living the high life. The truth was far from it—instead, we literally were high, and miles from being well off financially. I remember multiple times looking around and thinking to myself, thinking out loud to God, and asking Him, "Is this it, Lord? Is this my life?" Every time I asked, I would hear Him say, "No. Why are you there? You put yourself there."

One day, after one of our biggest fights, I ran into the house to where my children were playing and began sobbing. I knew I had to stop, not just for myself but for my children. I was neglecting my little girls, for what? For something that was only making me happy temporarily. The laughter only lasted in that moment— once the hit was gone, it was back to reality where arguments, abuse and selfish ambitions came first. It was financially, mentally, and physically draining and my children did not deserve to come second.

I know everyone's road to recovery is different, and it's absolutely not easy. My own journey was incredibly difficult. I made a conscious decision to give up, then faced temptation and gave in, but I also learnt from my failures. This was something I couldn't do on my own. Every time I tried to do it in my own strength I would only get so far before stumbling back to my addiction. I had to bring God into my recovery and find like-minded people. It was a daily battle! At that point, I was still with Marc, so that temptation was always present. I had to take one day at a time and couldn't get ahead of myself. I did not trust myself, but I trusted God. He placed the people I needed around me, He blessed me with a job which helped us financially, and eventually He gave me the confidence and motivation I needed to end that relationship.

If you're in a position where you feel all is lost and you are trapped, please do not give up! If you haven't tried recovery with God, give it a go. You never know what will happen. At the time, I was a huge mess. I was lost, I was broken. I was a sinner . . . I still am. If He can help me, He will definitely help you. God loves you the way you are, and takes you as you are. You just have to be willing.

So, are you willing?

8

A New Start

And we know that God causes everything to work together for the good of those who love God and are called according to his purpose for them.

Romans 8:28, NLT

Three years after I finally separated from my partner, God brought another man into my life, although I had stopped going to church by then, and at the time I wasn't giving God much thought. I met Teariki online and we starting talking to each other before we decided to meet up. At first, it was meant to be a bit of fun. Neither of us wanted our relationship to be serious, but that soon changed when I found out I was pregnant. We were both surprised. Our relationship was still very new and we certainly hadn't thought it through, but we decided to move in together and give it a go. It wasn't easy, especially because Teariki now had to take on the responsibility for my two girls as well as our soon-to-be-born son. Thankfully, Teariki had a job, so both of us were working, and we began to make plans to stay together and build a family of our own.

We were going to be parents! Neither of us were born again at the time, but God does not leave us in the state He found us in. By the time I was seven months pregnant with my fourth child, we had savings, we had a good house, and we had everything we wanted. And yet I wasn't happy. I knew I was missing something.

One day I was at home, sitting on the bed thinking about things when I had something like a lightbulb moment—a voice telling me that what I was missing was Jesus. For the next two weeks, I started doing daily devotions and reading my Bible. Teariki noticed a change in me—he saw that I was spending time reading the Bible and asked me if I was okay. In fact, he asked me if I was happy. I replied that yes, I was happy, but there was something that I was missing. Teariki was okay with that. I told him that I was going to start going back to church, and that I would be taking the children with me—that I was going, with or without him. I was surprised when he replied, "Okay, I'll come with you."

Together we looked online to find a church near us, and the next Sunday we all went to church. I was nervous as we headed into the service. I didn't know what was going to happen, but I knew it was going to be a good thing, and we started going to church every Sunday.

It was during a service about a month later, that my heart starting beating hard out. I remember thinking that it wasn't particularly hot, but I was sweating. I felt uncomfortable, but in a good kind of way. I knew it was the Holy Spirit stirring me up. As the pastor spoke, it was as if the message was only for me. That day, when the pastor offered to lead people in prayer, I lifted up my hand and asked God to come into my life.

At the time, Teariki didn't know what to make of it all, but he liked being at church and finally, in a similar service a few years later, he also gave his heart to the Lord. The preacher talked about being halfway through a door—not fully in or out—and when he invited people to come to Christ, Teariki put his hand up. I didn't realise Teariki had responded until after the service, and when I heard that he too had decided to follow Christ, I was speechless, in awe of God! I could hardly believe it. This was a huge answer to prayer! With our new life and new hope, we began growing in our faith together.

9

Giving Up Control

> *And a small rudder makes a huge ship turn wherever the pilot chooses to go, even though the winds are strong. In the same way, the tongue is a small thing that makes grand speeches.*
>
> James 3:4-5, NLT

When I returned to the Lord, He still accepted me, all of me. The 'everything' I came with, He took it all and restored every part of me. That's the beauty of who Jesus is—He never turns anyone away, no matter what they've done or been through. He took me in His loving arms and to this day, He's never let me go! But the way I had been living had a far-reaching affect.

When I first met Teariki, I found it hard to be a team-mate and get alongside him. I refused to let him lead. A part of me didn't know how

GIVING UP CONTROL

to. I had always hated being told what to do, and struggled to listen to alternative ideas. Maybe this is because I carried the responsibility for being the 'head of the family' for so long. I had made the decisions and been the provider for years, and to let someone else take those roles was difficult. Two people can't lead at the same time! But there I was, trying anyway. I wanted to be in control.

Being a leader comes naturally to Teariki, but I didn't notice at first. My stubbornness blinded me from seeing what God was trying to do in our family—He was putting order back into our home and into my relationship with Teariki. I had to let him lead and make decisions, but most of all I had to simply learn how to keep my mouth shut. I had something to say in response to everything! Teariki would give up trying because my mouth was so persistent. My words got in the way and my partner's great ideas were forgotten because I didn't respect and trust him to make decisions for us. It's true—the tongue is the smallest muscle in the body, but spits out the most powerful words!

But it wasn't merely learning to submit to Teariki that was needed—I had to hand over ultimate control to God, and trust Him to lead Teariki too. It was overwhelming surrendering it all, like handing over the keys of a brand-new, uninsured car to an unlicensed driver. There is no guarantee the car would return in the same condition in which you bought it, or that the driver could be trusted to keep it that way.

I wasn't forced to hand over the 'keys of control'. I could've said no and continued to fight for dominance, both with Teariki and with God. I had to hand it over freely, with no 'ifs' and 'buts', no negotiating, no terms and conditions. I had to remember all the times God was faithful, when He provided our family with what we needed, when He kept me safe and protected me in a violent relationship, and the times that my children were sick and He healed them. All those moments when He was faithful were more than enough for me to trust Him with guiding Teariki and my family. By handing over control, it created room for God to move in our family and in Teariki's life, and it was good!

Since returning to the Lord, I have had to unlearn and relearn so many things. Letting go of what we think we know, or things we've clung to, is not easy. In fact, it is downright scary. Now, as a mum, I had to learn to trust Him with my children too.

This is a reality that every mum can take hold of. Putting God first in my life means trusting Him enough to let go of my circumstances and do things His way! Proverbs 3:5-6 says, "Trust in the Lord with all your heart and lean not on your own understanding; in all your ways submit to him, and he will make your paths straight."

10

Dying to Self

> *"If anyone desires to come after Me, let him deny himself, and take up his cross, and follow Me. For whoever desires to save his life will lose it, but whoever loses his life for My sake will find it."*
>
> Matthew 16:24-25, NKJV

I wear many hats in my life—wife, daughter, sister, aunty, niece—but most of all, I am a mother. I now have six children, two from my previous relationship, and four with Teariki. Teariki and I have been together for seven years now, but I feel like I've known him forever! Those are my most precious relationships, but before those comes my relationship with God.

The words Jesus spoke to His disciples in Matthew 16 form the very foundation of what it means to be a follower of Christ. Jesus makes it clear; you can live for yourself and save your own life, but in the process, you will lose it. It's the same for all of us.

Instead, every day I have to die to myself. The things I want and think I need, I have to give up because it's not about me. It's not about any of us—it's about what Christ wants us to do, daily. Certainly, there are days where I don't put Him first because I let the busyness of life get in the way. Living for Christ is a daily sacrifice. Every morning we must choose to live in righteousness. When you wake up, you have the choice to love your children, you have the choice to love your partner, you have the choice to go to work. It's the same with choosing God every day. Jesus laid down His life for us. In turn, we get to lay down our lives for the people we love.

What it means to put God first will look different for each of us. For me, it revolves around spending time with Him—when I wake and before I sleep every day—through prayer, personal devotions, and in praise and worship. I know sometimes the last thing you want to do after a rough day is spend time with God. Household chores pile up, time slips away, and before you know it, it is time for bed! So, I challenge you to try focusing on the morning. Getting up before your household awakens, and spending time with God will set the tone for your day and it prepares your heart, creating space for growth and maturing.

For me, that is mothering and parenting my children the way God wants me to. Being a mum is the hardest thing I've ever had to do, but every day He gives me what I need to love and care for my children, and to put them before myself. Dealing with the tantrums, the sibling rivalry, the fighting and the moaning is a battle in itself, but in all the chaos, God's Word always gives me peace and the power to persevere.

His Word is my therapy. It's okay not to have your life planned out, it's okay not to wash or brush your hair every day, it's okay to skip household chores and let the laundry pile up. It's okay! There are more important things than those mundane activities.

I used to panic and get grumpy when the house wasn't in order—honestly, that behaviour was ugly! When I started to put God first, He showed me that I was missing out on my children. I needed to be 'in the moment'. I was physically there, but I was not actively present and never showed interest in what my children were doing. I needed to take the love God has for me and show it to my children through how I parent them, discipline them, talk to them and even how I listen to them. It's not easy, and I am still learning—because this mothering gig never ends. Even when they grow up and move out of home, they will always be your children and you will always be their mother.

If you're like me and struggle with dying to yourself daily, I hope that you also remember the sacrifice God made for us by letting His only Son, Jesus, die on the cross for us. He was severely beaten, bruised, ridiculed, and mocked for us, for you, so that your sins could be forgiven. I now have two sons, and I could not imagine losing them—or any of my children. It would break my heart. But God gave up His Son for you and me. I don't know about you, but I think that's pretty amazing!

11

Who's the Breadwinner?

*Do not use your freedom to indulge the flesh;
rather, serve one another humbly in love.*

Galatians 5:13

When Teariki and I first started dating I viewed love totally differently from how I do now. Our relationship hasn't been perfect—far from it, actually—but one thing I know is that we truly love each other. Looking back, I can see I didn't know what love was, or how to love anyone other than my children. I love my children unconditionally and they love me back, regardless of how much I screw up. When it came to other relationships, it wasn't so clear-cut.

At the start of our relationship, I thought loving Teariki was shown through sexual performance, or acts of service—cleaning the house, cooking dinner, doing his laundry. I thought I could demonstrate it through doing something for him that I knew he would like, and I thought sex was the answer. I knew I had brought my problems and issues from my previous relationship into this one, but decided not to let them affect us—it was time for me to be mature. It wasn't fair on Teariki to have to put up with my baggage and outbursts of insecurity.

I was learning to let him lead, but as more children came along, I found it difficult to give up being the breadwinner in the relationship. It was like giving the power to someone else, and it was a very difficult thing to do. Teariki is a hard worker, and always has been. He has the biggest heart, a giving heart, which is completely the opposite to me. When our son was born, we were both working. If he got sick one of us had to stay home, to sacrifice a day at work, and of course without discussion it was always me. I hated it! I always had something to say—*Woe is me!*

At the time, I didn't realise what God was trying to tell me. I can see now how He was showing me that my first priority is to be a mother. God has different ways of speaking to us individually and it took me a long time to realise this calling over my life. When I did, I decided to give up my job and be a stay-at-home mum. I learnt to support my partner's decisions, to follow his lead, and to be completely honest I'm still learning this. As the years pass, God is taking my understanding of love and flipping it upside down, completely blowing my mind.

One part of relationships I hadn't really considered was being a teammate. My previous relationships were anything but teamwork, but as I've grown as a follower of Christ, I have seen the merit in getting alongside my husband. We call it being 'partners' for a reason, after all!

Our teamwork was put to the test when Teariki left his job. It was a good job, he had a company car, and the payrate was above average. But he saw no room for future growth and felt the need to leave. Driven by fear of the unknown, I asked thousands of questions—some would call it nagging—but after all of that I had to step back and support his decision. I needed to cheer him on and encourage him as he led our family down a new path.

Teariki didn't leave his old job in order to do nothing. He is a planner. He thinks ahead, he steps out in faith (whereas I don't like to), and he learns as he goes. I, on the other hand, tend to overthink and over-analyse situations. As the years went by, Teariki definitely learnt from his mistakes but so did I. I learnt how to follow, and I learnt how to trust him. We struggled financially for years but God always managed to work through Teariki to provide for us.

I'm so thankful that today we are financially stable to a degree that might never have happened if I hadn't stepped back to let him be the man, the head of our family. I would have manipulated every decision he was trying to make, and that isn't love. Love doesn't control. Love does not come with an agenda. I always expected something in return, but love does not.

Each of us does this differently. For me it was wanting to be right and in charge: "I did this and that for you, so you need to listen me," or "Show me you love me by doing what I say." This is a very carnal way of operating; it is controlling and ugly. God taught me the true definition of what love is, and showed me through my husband. This love is so much more than the love Teariki has for me or what I have for him.

Of course, I'm not advocating for submitting to someone who is abusive and wants to control you for their own ends. There is nothing godly about that! Following a good, God-honouring leader, a trustworthy teammate that you can get alongside, and working together with them is something quite different. Spouses who live in that kind of unity shine God's light out into the world in a beautiful and unusual way.

Whether we are parenting alone, co-parenting, or raising our children together with our partner, life has twists and turns. Perhaps you, too, will face an unexpected pregnancy, a surprise diagnosis, or a financial crisis. No matter what life brings our way, we are not thrown off course. We do not lose our balance. Grounded in God's Word, and in our prayerful relationship with Him, our 'Mum-life' has a certainty I once never thought possible. You may think your particular circumstances leave you beyond help, but I can testify that God is good and He is faithful. He has loved us with an everlasting love, and He is more than sufficient to meet all our needs.

12

Identity

For you formed my inward parts; you covered me in my mother's womb.

Psalm 139:13, NKJV

Who am I? I spent many years searching for an answer to this question. I have only recently been able to say that I truly know who I am, and who God intended me to be. For the longest time, I searched for answers, for connections, for people to love me for who I was—but how could I find those things without knowing myself? The more I searched, the more lost I became. I have discovered that if we do not have a strong sense of identity and worth, society will decide them for us.

There are many opportunities in this world that distract you from becoming who God intended you to be. There is so much which can

IDENTITY

throw you off track, and boy, did it ever throw me off! The mentality of living 'in the moment' had me making decisions and doing things without really thinking of the consequences. I was driven by selfish ambition. The relationships I had were built on false truths. I didn't love the person I was, nor who I was becoming.

I used to think my culture and nationality defined me, and I relied on traditions to shape me into the person I was meant to be. I would try to act more Samoan or more Māori when I was around certain people in order to feel a sense of identity and worth. The reality is, there is only One who can form your identity. No culture or person can tell you who you are! You are who God says you are!

When I became a mother, I believed the negative words that were spoken over me. I settled for less in order to keep safe. Fear clouded my judgement and held me back from exploring and finding out who I truly was. It wasn't until I recommitted my life to Christ that I started to realise that I am so much more than my mind can even comprehend.

I knew I had to remove everything in my life that did not align with God. Two of the major things that I had to change were how I thought and how I talked about myself. As a mother it breaks my heart hearing one of my children speaking negatively about themselves and the way they look. Imagine how God feels when we His children do the same. Like the good Father He is, He is always speaking the truth over us. I would always reassure my children that they're beautiful or handsome and perfect in every way, but I couldn't say that to myself. I was my biggest critic! I judged myself; I hated the way I looked. What I saw in the mirror I considered ugly. The thoughts I had weren't of God. The enemy was trying to stop me from walking in my true identity.

For many years I tried to be someone other than myself. I compared myself to other people—what people look like, the jobs they have, the friends in their circle, how they dress and how they speak. I was always trying to be everyone else except myself. Why? Because I didn't know who I was in Christ.

Honestly speaking, I never loved myself. I tried to cover it up by the way I dressed. I always made sure I looked presentable and put together, like nothing was wrong, no part of my life was out of line. In reality, my life was a mess! I never liked my hair, I wished it was curly or straight. I wished I was skinny. I was obsessed with my body image and fixated on doing regular workouts. I grew up being told that God loves me, that I'm unique—there's only one me. It's one thing to say such things, but to truly believe it is a different story.

In order to find out who I truly was, I had to know what God said about me. I had forgotten the reason why my mother took us to church every Sunday, why she made us pray and learn the Lord's Prayer—it was to know Jesus! It was to know I wasn't defined by my past or by the negative opinions of others, but by God. I am a princess, a daughter of the King! And I had to start thinking like one. Once I understood this, I started to love myself and who I was. I'm not perfect, and I still do things I shouldn't do. I know I annoy some people but my personality, my flaws, and my weaknesses were no mistake. Those things all make up 'me'.

I can now say I am defined by Christ's love. He has made me the person I am today. I am the best mother, wife, aunty, sister, and friend that I can be because of the love God has for me. Because I know who I am in Christ, my thoughts and everything I do is aligned with who God has said I am. I can live my life in freedom and peace. A huge weight has finally been lifted off my shoulders. God has called me out

IDENTITY

of darkness into His wonderful light.

So, *who am I?*

I am a child of God, I am a princess, a daughter of the King, and I am worthy!

13

Discover your Beauty

> *I am fearfully and wonderfully made;* **marvelous are Your works**, *and that my soul knows very well. My frame was not hidden from You when I was made in secret, and* **skilfully wrought** *in the lowest parts of the earth. Your eyes saw my substance, being yet unformed, and in Your book they all were written,* **the days fashioned for me***, when as yet there were none of them.*
>
> Psalm 139:14-16, NKJV

It's easy to read words like 'marvellous are your works' as if they're saying, "You're so good, God. Look at how beautiful the skies and the mountains are. Thank you, Lord, for creating such beauty!" But do we ever stop to thank God or glorify Him for making such beauty as you and me? Have you? Because I never did! I never saw it like that. I never asked God to reveal the beauty He placed within me.

DISCOVER YOUR BEAUTY

Psalm 139:15 tells us we are 'skilfully wrought'. 'Wrought' means 'moulded, shaped, or manufactured'. In other words, God is saying that He crafted you, gazing at you from every possible angle until He had you just right. He skilfully took His time in creating you.

The following verse speaks of 'the days fashioned for me'. This speaks volumes to me, and should to you as well. I wasn't merely designed to know who I am, but why I am here. God predestined, planned out, the days I'm going to live out on this earth. God makes no mistakes! I am not a mistake and you are not a mistake! Everything about yourself that you view as an error, your flaws, the things you hate or haven't accepted, these things are no mistake!

We are all made differently. Your molecules, fingerprints, ears, eyes, everything about you is unique. Therefore, you are made perfectly as God intended! No human can ultimately tell you who you're meant to be or give you the value you desire, only God can do that. He's the Creator of all things, and He gives us purpose, so you should ask the Creator about His plans for your life!

When I was young, I thought my purpose was to work in the mental health sector as a support worker. I studied while working and then tried to find a job but wasn't successful. Many years later, I finally asked God what *He* wanted me to do. He said to try again, so I did. I applied, and two weeks later I had a job as a mental health support worker. It felt awesome to be working and contributing financially like many other women I knew.

Three months into the new job I found out I was pregnant with my sixth child. I was not happy! I thought to myself, "No! Not again Lord!" I love my children, but I love to work as well. But now with five children and the sixth on the way, I saw no hope for me. I saw having that many children as failure. I had always said I loved being a mother, but in reality I always saw it as a chore. Don't get me wrong, I love my children. I knew there had to be a deeper reason for why I was feeling this way.

I came to realise that it was to do with my own mother. I had seen her struggle financially, and I knew that she had wanted to be more than 'just a mother', even though she had known it was only for a season. I saw how my mother had lived and knew I wanted more for my life. I did everything possible to not be like her. I still had a worldly mindset of what a person should and shouldn't be doing. My view was one where we are defined by our occupation, what qualifications we have, how much money we make and what we possess.

At the time I did not realise my children were the very reason I was here. I did not know that my current purpose was related to what I'm doing right now—which is simply being a mother. Perhaps new purposes will be revealed to me in the future, but for now, being a mother is my God-given assignment. I have to admit I found this the hardest thing to accept. It was only through God's reassurance to form my identity in Him that I have been able to do so.

I wish I had been given this advice as a teenager:

> *To find your purpose and what you're created for, you need to ask the One who created you.*

Now that I know this, I love the role that I'm living out. I love being a mother and all that means—showing the love of God to my children through how I live, how I discipline them, talk to them and care for them. Everything I do needs to reflect God's love. I can wholeheartedly say I love being a mother. I know I'm a great mother. Even when I fall short, I know God has my back and fills in that gap. I don't care about others' opinions and what they say about me. He appointed me to be the mother to my children and I will do it well.

As God reveals who we truly are, piece by piece, we are confronted with sin. That can be painful and discouraging, but God, in His kindness, shows us these things so that we can move forward into freedom and the fullness of joy. This not only enables us to love ourselves more, and walk without fear or hiding, but we also get to love those around us, and God, more fully. As mums, this divine clean-up of our lives gives us the opportunity to show our children what it looks like to walk fully freed, and to teach them to do the same. The old is gone, the new has come!

14

The Power of Porn

> *Do not conform to the pattern of this world, but be transformed by the renewing of your mind. Then you will be able to test and approve what God's will is—his good, pleasing and perfect will.*
>
> *Romans 12:2*

Everyone thinks watching porn is a thing only males do. Well, it's not! Females are right there with them. I know. I was one of them.

As a teenager, sex was the main attraction in most of my relationships. It was the foundation; everything was built on sex. I was exposed to porn once and was instantly hooked! I thought 'one time won't hurt' but little did I know. I became a slave to it. No matter how hard I tried, I couldn't stop. I had no self-control. Porn led to self-pleasure and it became frequent to a point where it was all I thought about. I justified it as normal, it made me feel good and I figured that was all that mattered. Deep down, however, I knew it was wrong. The habit had its claws deep into me, and it was desperately difficult to stop. I realised the only way I could shake this addiction was by thinking differently. I only masturbated when I wanted to feel good, so I needed to stop focusing on my feelings.

Even in later years as a Christian I was attending church but watching porn in my spare time. I was ashamed! It's definitely not Christian behaviour and it's not something the church talked about either. I was afraid to share because of how people might react and treat me if they knew. It was my shame that kept me in bondage.

Only by trusting God did I find true freedom from this shame. With His help I was able to open up and share with other women, and surprisingly I found some were experiencing the same struggle. To me that was proof we don't go through anything alone. That we are isolated in our sin is a lie we tell ourselves. My life group from church was a place where I could be honest about what triggered me to turn to both porn and sex. For me, the most common trigger I found was easy access! There are so many dating apps available online you don't even have to go far searching; it's all at the tip of your finger. Based on someone's profile picture, you either swipe left (not interested), or right (yes please). These apps openly promoted sex and I believed it was okay because the apps are legal. If it was harmful, it wouldn't be available, right? Wrong. Just because it is there does not mean it's good for you and you should use it. Soon I found that even watching a movie with sex scenes would trigger me. It got so bad I didn't need to watch porn to get started, and this led to me start sleeping around.

It was my loneliness that triggered the temptations, particularly when I first arrived back from Australia. I thought I could shake the addiction by having an intimate relationship. I went looking in the wrong places for it. I was looking for love and, in my desperation, slept with a married man. I thought sex and love were the same thing but they most definitely are not. I didn't know that God designed sex for married couples. When they become one flesh, it's sacred!

Looking back now, I can see I was very immature. Every relationship I had was broken because I was broken. I was focused on myself instead of being focused on God, the only One who can set anyone free and break the habit of addiction. The only love we truly need is that which only God can give, His pure love for you and me. Sex is different—it can be an expression of love, but it can also be an addiction, and like any addiction, sometimes the symptoms are visible and sometimes, they are not. If you knew me when I first became a mum, you would've never known because I hid it so well. It affected my mental state as I always thought about it, and it affected my children because I neglected them at night to go and satisfy my sexual urges. Not the proudest moments in life, but I am proud of who I've become now. Jesus has truly set me free! Now, He is my foundation! He is the one I turn to, and every time without fail I find happiness, peace, joy, and love!

The hurt, the abuse, the addiction, God uses it all—it is not to be hidden or to be ashamed of. It is to be shared to help others. These are moments that I am not proud of—but they are real. By God's grace, my past has not held me back from becoming the woman and mother that I am now. He renews our minds!

The Bible warns us that sin is crouching at the door, but that we must master it (Genesis 4:7). Thankfully, Jesus gives us the power to face whatever temptations might come our way. In our own strength, this is not possible, but in His, we can turn away from evil and into His light. Our children will face the world and its trials too. Let us not be naïve about this, but instead prepare them for what they might face, give them the tools to deal with it, and let them know that God is able to deliver them from every area of bondage.

As mothers, we have the privilege and opportunity to raise our children with the knowledge of where to turn when things get tough! Let us show them that they can always come to Mum for help, for a listening ear, and for a prayer warrior who will carry their troubles to God, knowing that He alone can set them free!

15

Dealing with Insecurity

*So do not throw away your confidence;
it will be richly rewarded.*

Hebrews 10:35

I'm thirty-four years old and still have moments when I feel insecure. As I've matured, I've learnt to get through those moments by refusing to give in to fear and facing challenges head on. Insecurity wears many different faces and although I only experienced a few, they affected me. "I'm not good enough," I always spoke over myself. "I'm not a good mother." "I'm not the prettiest woman so I'm not good enough for my partner." "I'm not smart and don't know big words—how will I write a book?!"

I never thought words could have such a devastating effect on my confidence. I never saw that the negative words I spoke over myself were keeping me from living up to my full potential. If anything, I am the total opposite of what I believed. God tells me I am good enough, that I am a fun and loving mother, that I am the best spouse, and guess what? I believe every word—it's the truth!

Growing up, we weren't rich, but we weren't poor either. My mother or older sister made sure we had everything we needed. When I hit adulthood however, I always wanted more. I was never satisfied. I always had to have, have, have! I compared myself to others. I wanted what they had, and I found myself taking a lot of things for granted. Bitterness and jealousy grew in my heart. I was disappointed with the life I had. I wanted what money couldn't buy—happiness and joy—and yet I was blind towards God.

I've learnt that when God wants to get your attention, He does so on a huge scale. God took everything I had, the material things I valued, friendships I took for granted, and multiple job opportunities and these slowly but surely disappeared. It's sad to lose everything, but the first person we need to turn to is God. He wanted me to value Him and love Him more than anything else. He wanted me to trust Him, to fully trust Him. But I had major trust issues. I trusted no one! Not even my siblings. How messed up was that? They are blood-related and yet I did not trust them. I didn't want to invest in any new relationships, especially with other women, whom I didn't trust at all. I was so scared of being hurt that I thought if I didn't get too deep in a friendship then I wouldn't be left disappointed if that relationship went sour. I could easily pull away like it meant nothing and keep my emotions under control.

The real issue was never other people though. The reality was, I couldn't trust myself. Insecurity kept me in bondage, but God wants us to walk in freedom. It takes a lot of conscious effort to rebuke the negative thoughts that infiltrate our minds, and declare God's truth over our lives. He says to love your neighbour as yourself, but how can we expect to obey those words if we don't even love ourselves?

We must first learn to trust what God's Word says about us. We must also make a choice to love ourselves despite how we may feel. When I decided to trust God and His words, I found His unconditional love was more than enough for me. If God loves me, then I am worth loving. What other confirmation do I need? I don't need to love myself because of the good things I do, but because He is good, and I am His creation. I am no mistake! You are no mistake! His love is freedom! You might be 'just a mum' but you are a great mother, and God has made you exactly right for your children!

16

Our Genealogy

You are a chosen people, a royal priesthood, a holy nation, God's special possession, that you may declare the praises of him who called you out of darkness into his wonderful light.

1 Peter 2:9

When I think about my genealogy, I think of my family and cultural background, where I come from. I didn't understand it when I was younger, but these are the things that keep me grounded. When I asked my family and friends what 'genealogy' means to them, I was amazed at the responses. Suddenly they started talking again about the generations that have gone before and also of their culture and country of origin.

My favourite genealogy is the genealogy we share in Christ. I believe genealogy in Christ is different to the genealogy in the world and its culture. The world makes everything about 'self' and the individual. It is filled with man-made rules and traditions ingrained within cultures making it difficult to ever break away and have your own opinion. Life in Christ, as part of His body, is dynamic—we have purpose and belonging beyond ourselves, but we're also set free to truly be ourselves!

My own ethnic background is one of a Māori and Samoan woman. My mother is part-Māori, and my father is Samoan. 'Plastic Māori' is the term they use here in New Zealand, or 'Afakasi' in Samoan, meaning 'half-Europeans'. These labels stuck with me throughout my teenage years. I never felt like I belonged to any culture. I did not identify myself as either culture—not because I was ashamed, but because I had no understanding of the importance of my cultural customs and practices—I couldn't see the significance.

Even though my mother and father were separated, my mother looked after a lot of my older cousins and I grew up surrounded by those from both my Māori and Samoan sides. Nearly all of my childhood memories include my cousins. Our house was never empty—I was always surrounded by family, yet I felt different to them. My siblings and I were brought up in a mainstream Christian church, whereas the majority of my cousins were taught the ways of the Rātana church in New Zealand. It was as if we drew our happiness, joy, and strength from separate sources. We were certainly not seen as the most acceptable of my extended family, and I couldn't quite capture why we felt so different. Having a contrasting understanding of life put a wedge between us.

I asked my mother how she became a Christian after having been brought up in the Rātana church. She said it was because of my grandfather. He used to take her to church with him. One day my mother heard her dad was going to an event where Billy Graham was one of the speakers. I remember her saying she never intended on going into the venue—she had planned to stay in the car—but something stirred inside of her, pushing her to go. At the exact moment when she finally walked in, Billy Graham was finishing his sermon and started giving the alter call. This was the moment she gave her heart to the Lord, and this was the start of our genealogy in Christ!

My grandfather laid that foundation for my mother and she for us, the next generation. Now as a mother myself, I'm trying to build on that very foundation my grandfather laid. It makes me wonder who introduced my grandfather to Christ? The possibilities are endless, but one thing I know—in Christ I have a long line of ancestors that reaches right back to Abraham! In Genesis 26:4, God promised Abraham he would have as many descendants as there are stars in the sky. That's a lot of people! Somehow, it was all part of God's divine plan, a plan that includes me and will extend down to my family.

Don't get me wrong, I'm proud to be both Māori and Samoan and there are still times when I find myself being 'big on culture'. But honestly, the only culture I really know and love is Kingdom-culture, the culture of God's children. As a child of God, everything that comes with Him is mine as well, and that includes the people who I do life with. I have family related by blood, and then I have family bound together by the blood of Jesus!

Kingdom culture is the culture I want my children to uphold, respect and love, just as much as I do. I love that we are not defined by our nationality, our ethnic background or the colour of our skin. We are defined by the blood of Jesus! And that's all you and I and my children need to know. We are His sons and daughters by blood!

17

Overcoming Loneliness

*God is our refuge and strength, an
ever-present help in trouble.*

Psalm 46:1

Have you ever been in a room full of people and still felt lonely? I have and it is really depressing. It's a horrible feeling! Being alone and being lonely are very different. 'Alone' describes a state of being, and 'lonely' describes an emotional response to one's circumstances. I love being alone! As a mum, having some time to myself is a miracle and I enjoy every moment of it when I need to refuel. In times like these, I am content because I know I won't be alone forever. However, there have been times in my life when I have experienced debilitating loneliness and I have learnt to overcome that in God's strength.

I remember one weekend when Teariki had to fly to Wellington for work. I thought nothing of it at first. It wasn't a big deal. I was actually really excited for him to be gone for a few days. I was looking forward to having our bed to myself. The afternoon he left, I was alone at home, pregnant with child number six, the kids were at school, and I had completed all the household chores when suddenly, this wave of loneliness rushed over me. At the time I didn't know what it was I was feeling. I had never experienced it before. Even though I'd been so looking forward to being alone, the majority of the time Teariki was away working I sat and I cried! I felt so alone, it was overwhelming.

During all the chaos and noise with the kids, all I wanted was to have Teariki home. I started to blame people for my loneliness. I became angry at Teariki for working away and not jumping on a plane immediately when I told him I missed him, and for not expressing how much he missed me. Ridiculous—I know! I was isolating myself without even realising it.

I used to be a person who didn't like to show my feelings. I didn't share anything that made me look weak to anyone, my partner included. It wasn't his fault I was angry and lonely, and yet I blamed him. Instead of communicating with him, I chose to ignore the fact that I was suffering and tried to disguise it. I hid it. I turned to social media, thinking if I killed time online, the days would pass faster. I saw it as a distraction from dealing with my feelings. Honestly, I didn't know any other way to handle my pain.

The truth is, we are hardwired to live in companionship and to have an intimate connection with people. When God created people, He saw that it was not good for us to be alone. The message here is not 'go and find yourself a partner'. I'm trying to emphasise that it is not good to be alone. In short, don't isolate yourself. Self-seclusion only magnifies your loneliness. This is especially true in relation to our parenting. Pretending we're fine and faking it is exhausting. Don't try and cover it up or mask it with something else, because this will not fill the void. As you lean into God, you will find Him to be your greatest helper. But He also gives us people to come alongside us. None of us are meant to walk our journey alone!

If you are a mum, I encourage you to find a small group of mums and connect with them on a heart level. Invest time in each other. Pray with each other, and for each other's kids. As you focus on helping someone else escape their own loneliness, it will take the focus off yourself. And as you press in to the presence of God, you will find that He is with you always!

In one of my devotions, I was asked to think about my life, especially the lonely times. I was asked the following questions, and now I ask you:

> *How would things be different if someone had reached out to you during your times of loneliness, making sure you never felt alone?*
>
> *How many people are wondering why you didn't do that for them?*
>
> *And who is the Friend that is always within reach?*

The past suffering we endured, the insecurity and the loneliness that we experience, none of that has to define us. When we begin a new life in Christ, all of those things move into the 'old life' category. Our new lives are characterised by the confidence that God gives us, the ever-present friend who will never leave us even when we are physically alone, and the assurance that one day, all things will be made new, and suffering will be no more.

As we parent our children, as we pray for them, as we walk alongside them, it is our privilege to model a born-again life. We can show them, "that was then, and this is now. I no longer walk in fear but trust God to carry me through." We can bear with our children in their own struggles, hopeful in the knowledge that God's got them, just as He had us, and will continue to carry both them and us. In this life, we may face troubles, but we don't face them alone. God is always with us!

Here is a promise from God to help you remember that you are never alone: "No one will be able to stand against you all the days of your life. As I was with Moses, so I will be with you; I will never leave you nor forsake you" (Joshua 1:5). He's always with you and He will never abandon you!

18

A Father's Love

The LORD your God in your midst, the Mighty One, will save. He will rejoice over you with gladness, He will quiet you with His love, He will rejoice over you with singing.

Zephaniah 3:17, NKJV

I grew up with an absent father—my relationship with him was not one that taught me the value of being a daughter. I did not trust him, and any interaction he had with me only ever felt like a token gesture. When I found out I was pregnant at the age of seventeen, I knew I didn't want my children to grow up under the same circumstances, so I stayed with Marc. I wanted Sophia and Phyllis to have a present father, even though the relationship we had was for all the wrong reasons and was doomed from the start.

I used to regret the decisions I made back then, but today as an adult (an older and much wiser one), I don't regret anything because it's a part of me. I know not to let the past have power over my emotions or my mind but instead let it fuel me to do better and make wiser decisions based on God's Word.

The core of human interaction is trust, and without it a relationship is empty. That's the feeling I experienced when my father tried having a heart-to-heart conversation with me—emptiness. There was no emotional attachment there for me to ever give him a chance to try mending what was broken. I did not respect him, and I did not want to. Even if I tried to listen or take in his advice, only anger built within me. This only grew as I saw the struggles and challenges my mother faced as a solo mum. I hated my dad for being absent, and more so for not helping out more. I could not understand how a person could have children and tell them he loves them, but never fully demonstrate that love to them.

This played a huge part in my feeling unwanted, rejected, and abandoned. I thought, if my own father didn't want me, then who would? Wasn't I enough for him to stay around? If he didn't truly love me, why would anyone else? I tried really hard to keep people around. For years I stayed in my abusive relationship because I wanted to be loved and I didn't want the shame of rejection over me. I carried this around from a very young age right up till I was a young mother.

It wasn't until I had more children that I realised I actually didn't hate my father, in fact I really did love him. As a parent myself, I put myself in my father's shoes. How would I feel if my children treated me how I treated my father? It would break my heart. Who was I to hold my anger and hate for my father? Who was I to judge him? I had done the exact same thing he had, slept around. I slept with a married man, and even though I was one of many women, I played a part in his marriage coming to an end. How could I be so selfish!? I had blamed my father for being absent and cheating on my mother, and that's where I believed the unwantedness, rejection and abandonment had stemmed from. But that bitter root went deeper still. It didn't stem from the absence of my father or the past, it actually came from not knowing who I was or the amount of value I have as an individual. Whether people like me or hate me, I needed to know that God continued to love me.

When I left Marc, I thought to myself, "Who would ever want to love someone with children? Who would love this broken vessel?" The answer is: God did. And because He loves me, flaws and all, I can love myself and know that I am wanted, I am worthy, I am valuable and I'm never alone. What He says about me is all that matters. Viewing things this way has helped me to forget the past and start working on renewing my relationship with my father.

Close friends have asked me if I forgive my father and I can say now, there was nothing actually to forgive him for. He did nothing wrong to me. The wrong he did was to my mother, and I know she has forgiven him. It's crazy to think how we can fall into this trap of hurt, blaming everyone who injured us. We all have a choice to forgive and forget, to have the self-control to move on and keep the past where it belongs . . . in the past.

Getting to that point did not happen overnight or within a week; it took years of being honest, sharing my experiences and submitting to God until finally I found freedom in God's love. If you're feeling how I felt, please don't let the unwantedness, rejection and abandonment of a person have such power over you! It's not a good enough reason to hold things against them, to hate them or carry that shame. They are heavy chains weighing you down and holding you back from living in freedom and happiness.

When I look back across my life before I came to live for God, I see a shell of the woman I am now. Then I was hiding, now I live boldly. Then, I was living in unrighteousness, now God is my strength, the One who enables me to do good day by day. It is an exciting prospect that I can teach my children from a young age to live authentically, as God created them to be. I can teach them not to be bound up in lies or burdened by circumstances but to walk in freedom, a generation who impact those around them.

19

A Change of Attitude

But God demonstrates his own love for us in this:
While we were still sinners, Christ died for us.

Romans 5:8

After many years of being separated and never having consistent contact with the girls, Marc eventually decided he wanted to be a part of the girls' lives. It was awesome at first, but that didn't last long. Soon it was anything but awesome. We had agreed that he would have the girls for one week during the school holidays, then bring them back home. But when the week was over, he never brought them back! Child Services got involved, and this began a long process where Teariki and I took him through the Family Courts in an attempt to regain full custody for the girls. Unfortunately, it didn't go the way I'd hoped. For the short-term, we were given shared custody and suddenly, he was

A CHANGE OF ATTITUDE

back to calling all the shots, and I was left with having the girls only for the weekend. This was my new world. It was heart-breaking!

By this time, my life revolved around all my children, and with the two girls not around, two pieces of my heart had been torn away. I had been their sole provider and carer and now I wasn't! After a long and challenging process, I won the battle, and gained full custody of the girls once more. My girls were finally home after being away for four, long months.

While going through this process, I began to ask God, "How do you love people who have hurt you and offended you?" His answer was gentle. First of all, I had to change my attitude towards Marc. I'd held a grudge against him for years and God revealed my heart and showed me that I'd never truly forgiven him. I was still angry at him. For many years I had done things for him, bought things he wanted and needed. I was angry at him for not doing the same for me. I had this mentality that he 'owed me', he took and never gave, and this had built up into a hardened heart and hatred toward him. It all stemmed from the thought of him not treating me with the same generosity I treated him with. But that's not what love is; love is unconditional.

I wanted to see Marc suffer. I wanted him to endure pain as payback for all the years of hurt. I wanted him to at least apologise to me, but the reality was I was never going to get an apology, and that was no excuse for staying in my anger. God doesn't wait for us to first apologise when we sin. God demonstrated that what we need to do in order for us to forgive, is to love with "His own love" (Romans 5:8).

I first had to learn how to accept God's love so I could reflect His love to others, including Marc, who had wronged me so badly. It's not the world's way but it's powerful. We reflect His love by the way we treat people, mirroring how God treats us—with compassion, kindness, humility, gentleness, and patience. 'His love' binds us all together and brings unity (Colossians 3:12-14). I had enough of living in hatred. God wanted me to live in peace . . . and I wanted it too.

I encourage you to dig a bit deeper and meditate on this scripture in Matthew 6:14-15: "For if you forgive men their trespasses, your heavenly Father will also forgive you. But if you do not forgive men their trespasses, neither will your Father forgive your trespasses" (NKJV).

20

Loving Difficult People

Love is patient, love is kind. It does not envy, it does not boast, it is not proud. It does not dishonor others, it is not self-seeking, it is not easily angered, it keeps no record of wrongs. Love does not delight in evil but rejoices with the truth. It always protects, always trusts, always hopes, always perseveres.

1 Corinthians 13:4-7

It's true that the people who are the closest to you are sometimes the hardest to love. My siblings know I love them dearly, and they also know they drive me crazy. We all get on one another's nerves, but if any of us were in trouble or needed help, we would all be there to support them no matter the circumstance. The love our Father has for us is like that. Actually, His love is so much more! I had chosen to forgive Marc and was learning to love my dad. Over time, however, I found myself resenting my mum.

Growing up, I remember my mother always being busy around the house with one thing or another. As a child, I never thought anything of her constant busyness, but now, as a mother myself, I know how hard it is to raise a family. The saying, "It takes a village to raise a child," is true! My mother was the one in her family who looked after all the nieces and nephews. My childhood memories included a lot of my older cousins living with us, and they still greatly esteem Mum for that.

With a growing family, I would often call on my mother, asking her to come for visits to help look after my children, especially if my partner was away working, or if I needed some personal time. The majority of the time, she would say yes, but as time went on, she said no more frequently. I understood that it was a big ask—my mum lived about six hours' drive away. But I found myself annoyed that she seemingly didn't want to be around her grandchildren—my nieces and nephews as well as my own children. After a while, with the fear of a covid outbreak, travel restrictions were put in place, and even if she wanted to come, it became impossible. I was heart-broken to think of our children growing up without her, but I cannot control anyone else. I can only control my own attitudes and actions. Now that I live even further away from my mum, I have finally learnt that I don't need to rely on anyone but God who promises to be our ever-present helper.

I'm so glad God challenged me to dig deeper. When He asked me why I was so angry at my mother I knew straight away my heart wasn't in the right place. I came to this conclusion; I was self-indulging. I only cared about myself. I wanted time away from my children and responsibilities. I allowed anger to take root in my heart and it became the driving force behind how I reacted. I became ignorant and self-seeking causing me to shut out all communication from my mother, which over time spread to my siblings.

Would I continue holding a grudge, or would I choose to love my mum unconditionally, as God loves me? Even now, when I find my anger getting in the way, God quickly reminds me of all the times she could have been mad with me and yet she still showered me with love, supported me in my toughest times, wiped my tears and hugged me for no particular reason. I now understand that after so many years of serving her own children, she has finally got a chance to live her own life. I've been selfish for so long! Now I'm glad my mum can enjoy planning her days and having time to herself.

The Bible makes it clear what love is and how we should live it out. Love is the very essence of who God is; for God is love. His characteristics and nature all reveal love. We can read more about this in 1 John 4:7-10:

> *Dear friends, let us love one another, for love comes from God. Everyone who loves has been born of God and knows God. Whoever does not love does not know God, because God is love. This is how God showed his love among us: He sent his one and only Son into the world that we might live through him. This is love: not that we loved God, but that he loved us and sent his Son as an atoning sacrifice for our sins.*

Through these verses, God gave me the wisdom to see that how I was reacting to my mother was unfair and completely wrong. He showed me I was being ungrateful, not just towards her, but in all my relationships. I was being selfish and took for granted what truly mattered. The nature of love is selfless and seeks the good of others, while I was only seeking what benefitted me at the time. I was wrong to think the worst of my mother.

I began to see that I had very little love in my heart, and what small amount there was, it was buried deep. You see, every time someone annoyed me, I had a choice, a choice to respond in a negative way or to respond in a positive way. This is reflected in the way I treat people I imagine like this: Every time I respond negatively, a piece of my heart fades away or is replaced with hardness, but if I respond in a positive way, my heart softens. Of course, I'm not perfect and can't respond positively in every situation. And that's okay! If I can get better at it then so can you. God is always on hand to help us move forward.

21

Forgiveness

> *Be kind to each other, tender hearted, forgiving one another, just as God through Christ has forgiven you.*
>
> Ephesians 4:32, NLT

As God began to heal my relationships, it soon reached to my new, extended family. My relationship with Teariki's immediate family hasn't always been smooth sailing. We've had our share of disagreements and arguments, some little and some that have been very testing, but I honestly appreciate who they are and everything they do for us and our children. I'm getting teary-eyed writing this because I can say I love them wholeheartedly. I couldn't say that before but now I can!

When I first met Teariki's family I felt right at home. They accepted me and my two girls like their own. In fact, for three years we lived with his parents, which wasn't the easiest decision for either of us, but in order to save money, we decided to do it. At the time my partner was working away from home. His shift involved two weeks away, then he would come home for his four days' rest, then off he went again. He did this for two years. Boy, that was hard, especially given we weren't in our own home!

I kept to myself and his parents kept to themselves; they stayed out of my way and I stayed out of theirs. One day was all it took to change everything. An argument broke out over something very small, and things quickly escalated! I felt attacked. We all said things that were hurtful and, because I was the 'in-law', I felt I was on the outside. Living in their home was hard after that. Without my partner's presence, it was very awkward, and the lack of personal space became unbearable all around. It totally sucked. That was not an easy time for any of us!

Looking back, I can take responsibility and admit that a lot of what happened was my fault. I knew better, but I chose to say words I cannot take back. You can never shove words back into your mouth, no matter how much you want to. That one argument completely changed my relationship with certain family members. For years, I didn't trust them, and actually hated them. As it ate away at me, I knew I had to forgive my in-laws!

Forgiveness is one of the hardest things we can ever do. That was certainly true for me! Naturally speaking, I'm the kind of person to hold on to the past, especially if I get badly hurt or my trust is taken for granted. I found it much easier to say "I'm sorry" than to actually say "I forgive you" to their face. But the real struggle was having to deal with the bitterness, hatred, anger, and jealousy I had built around my heart like a wall. Why was it so hard for me to forgive?

FORGIVENESS

The truth is, I didn't even know how to forgive, or where to start, so I asked God to show me. That's when He led me to Ephesians 4:32. There I was quickly reminded of what Jesus had done for me—He died on the cross! He sacrificed Himself for me and you, so that our sins could be *forgiven*. If He could forgive and love my in-laws, then so could I! It's that simple. We are the ones who make it complicated and start adding the buts and what-ifs.

My mother once told me that forgiving someone isn't for the person receiving forgiveness, nor for them to give it back in return—it's for yourself, so you can walk around free and happy. No person should ever rob you of your joy and happiness! I've learnt that, as a mother myself, I need to set the example for my children, being the bigger person and taking the first step to saying sorry.

Relationships are hard, there is no doubt about that. Our relationships with our children, while beautiful, are no less challenging. We all have rough days, and moments when we speak harshly, saying things we regret. As mothers who love God and walk in His ways, we have a unique opportunity to model positive relationships to our children. We can exemplify relationships characterised by forgiveness and humility. We can show our children that when we make mistakes or when others sin against us, we have the tools to deal with it. We can pray in front of our children, ask our children for forgiveness when we wrong them, and teach them how to seek forgiveness from others. If we come from backgrounds where this is not the norm, we get to be those who break the cycle of unforgiveness and set a new pattern for future generations. We set the rules for how interactions go in our home: "As for me and my house, we will serve the Lord" (Joshua 24:15, NKJV). God has given us a new way of living, and it is our privilege to walk in it.

22

Solo Parenting

> *"Come to me, all you who are weary and carry heavy burdens, and I will give you rest."*
>
> Matthew 11:28, NLT

Life is full of unexpected moments, mundane moments, and beautiful, challenging, frightening and exhilarating moments. You never quite know what could be around the corner! Motherhood especially is like that—you think you've got a plan sorted, and then a lamp gets smashed, the baby has an explosion, or someone has a meltdown. What sets Christian mums apart is that we have a solid rock to stand on when the 'crazy' starts to happen. No matter the circumstances, we always have hope. We have a future to look to when things seem bleak. As followers of Christ, we get to live our everyday life in an extraordinary way.

I give it up to solo mothers who are taking care of business! You are doing the hardest thing in the world, raising children and doing it alone, without the father around. I was a solo mother as well and know exactly how challenging it is. The most frustrating and heart-breaking thing for me was hearing them cry out for their father. "Where's Daddy? When is Daddy coming home?" I would tell them that he wasn't here or that he was living somewhere else, thinking it would silence their crying. Instead they would get louder. If you're experiencing that now, let me tell you, it will get easier! Just like you, they need time to adjust. Give yourself space to breathe. At the end of the day, a solo mum is still a mum, and that's okay!

Being a solo mother and raising two children on my own had its moments. I couldn't go out since I had no babysitter and I hated asking my mother. If I wanted something done then I had to find a way to do it myself. If my children needed new clothes or shoes, I had to scrimp and save money. The struggle was real! I found it hard to find a job as day care was expensive, and it still is, but they didn't have the free hours available then. I also hadn't worked in years so I was concerned that no one would look at my resume and think, 'she's the one'.

I didn't give up though. Instead I decided to study mental health. While studying, I spent some time with the Lord, asking Him, "Is this all I'm supposed to do? This isn't going to pay for childcare or the things my children desperately need!" And, I prayed for a job. I had nothing to lose, so why not?

God's always listening, and when we least expect something to happen, it does. I got offered a job by a friend who worked for an organisation run by the church. They offered alternative education to young teens who had been kicked out of school. They were the teenagers who fell through the cracks of the education system. It was a huge blessing! As a teacher aide, I progressed to helping out in the youth prison and the Care and Protection facilities in South Auckland. This was a leap in responsibility, and with it came a jump in my hourly pay rate. I could not believe it! Once again, God had provided for me. I did not have to do anything—it all came to me. I was finally able to afford the things my girls needed, and much more!

Although God found me a job and provided financial stability in miraculous ways, I will never forget my past. I was on the sole parent benefit for years, comfortable at home, doing the same thing every day and waiting for pay day to arrive. These seasons aren't forever, and there is beauty in praising God from the hard places.

My mother was also a solo mother and took on the role of both parents. She took in some of my cousins and looked after them too. I remember asking her a few years ago how she did it, how she managed to take care of us all. She spoke about how God always provided for us. We weren't rich and we weren't poor, but I remember having everything I needed. My mother did not work, she was a stay-at-home mother. The memories I have of her are the best because she was always around; she always gave and found a way for my siblings and I to have the things we needed. If this isn't proof that God provides then I don't know what else to say, because He truly does! Knowing that my own mother made it through these rough times gave me hope that God would carry me through too, and even as a solo parent, that I could also provide a stable, loving home for my children, centred on God.

I now realise that God used solo-motherhood to sort my priorities out. They were all over the place and He showed me it was time for that to change. I didn't know what this looked like, but I knew my first priority had to be Him—before my children, before my finances, even before myself. I found this so difficult because my 'flesh' fights against it. The things I naturally wanted to do did not always align with God's way. I have to resist. Every day is a constant battle with myself. If I try to do it in my own strength, I will never make it through, but with God's enabling, I am able to succeed in following His calling for me. Being a solo mum is never an easy journey, but placing God in His rightful place in your life changes everything. He provides much more then we can ever imagine or dream!

23

Enjoying Motherhood

*And He said to me, "My grace is sufficient for you, for
My strength is made perfect in weakness." Therefore
most gladly I will rather boast in my infirmities, that the
power of Christ may rest upon me.*

2 Corinthians 12:9, NKJV

When I discovered I was pregnant with our sixth child I was not happy. I cried for two days. I was already in over my head. I found the responsibilities of five children overwhelming. How could I cope with yet another added to the mix? I couldn't get out of my head. I refused to attend to my children's needs, I didn't want to clean or cook, shower, or talk to anyone. I really was having a pity party and I was the only one attending.

Thinking back, I was such a sook! I had been convinced I was going to have no more children. I had made plans to return to work, contribute to our savings to buy a house and be that working mother, but God had other plans for me. If it wasn't for God moving through Teariki in that time, I would still be in that state of mind. I couldn't understand how this baby was going to be a blessing, because all I was thinking about was myself. Thankfully, the love and patience my partner showered me with made me realise my attitude sucked! I wanted to be left alone, I needed space, and on the other hand, I didn't want to be by myself—it was truly messed up. My selfishness was clouding my vision, but I soon realised that I couldn't continue feeling sorry for myself with children and a partner who needed me. I had to be honest about my situation and stop seeing my new circumstances as an obstacle. I needed to accept that my days might not get easier, but that I could rise up as a mum and choose life for my unborn baby—and life for myself! I needed to face the reality that each day is what I make of it, seeking joy rather than trying to escape my situation, and choose to be grateful for what God had given me.

The nine months of my sixth pregnancy were no walk in the park. I had more moments where I complained, moaned, and cried about everything. It truly was a long period of suffering for Teariki and our children. I had to rewire my mind, quit my whinging and start thinking positively. The first and last trimester were the hardest, but as the birth came closer, I found myself surrendering and laying everything at God's feet more than any time in my life so far.

I learnt to take one day at a time. I chose to make it enjoyable, to press into God daily despite being tired. I had to stop comparing myself to other mothers and women who weren't pregnant, who could fit their clothes, didn't have swollen feet, who could go to the gym or walk like a normal person without the waddling thing going on. I was too busy thinking that everyone else was living the dream to see the fact that I was living someone else's dream.

It was during that pregnancy that God made me realise how blessed I actually am. There are women out there who desperately want children of their own but can't have any. I knew I had to let God be in control and embrace this situation with an open heart. I had to humble myself, repent and admit that I couldn't do it in my own strength. I had already tried living in my own strength and I was left with stress, exhaustion, and unhappiness. With God's empowerment, my burdens become lighter.

"My strength is made perfect in weakness" (2 Corinthians 12:9). This scripture helped me get through so many ugly situations, both the big and the small. God's grace is more than enough for every difficult time we will ever go through, even if it doesn't seem possible. Our weakest moments are where we find His strength if we need it and seek it. You will find rest in Him!

24

Life with Christ

> *We do not wrestle against flesh and blood, but against principalities, against powers, against the rulers of the darkness of this age, against spiritual hosts of wickedness in the heavenly places.*
>
> Ephesians 6:12, NKJV

I have learnt that there is an enemy, and it's not someone who mistreats you or a person you don't like. Behind every evil and ugly thing there is one being who is ultimately responsible and that is the devil, Satan. I encourage you to learn the strategies of Satan. A key in helping understand his tactics is realising that the devil knows you even better than you know yourself. He knows what triggers you, what tempts you, what has worked in the past, and he's not afraid to push you past your limit to lead you back into sin.

We discover a little of Satan's playbook in 1 John 2:16: "For all that is in the world—the lust of the flesh, the lust of the eyes, and the pride of life—is not of the Father but is of the world" (NKJV). This verse lists three temptation tactics that Satan uses. The first is the lust of the flesh. It will look different to everyone depending what our heart desires.

In Luke 4:3-5, Satan tempts Jesus by saying He should turn a stone into bread. Jesus was in the wilderness for forty days where He ate nothing. Could you imagine going forty days without food? I can't go without food for two days! Jesus would've been starving, and Satan tempted Him to sin by offering a way to satisfy His craving.

He does this to us as well. Satan tells you that you need something in order to be satisfied, a temporary fix. This temptation usually pops up when we're struggling with obedience and starting a task God has given us to do. I personally struggle with going shopping and spending money. I'm so focused on what I want sometimes that I forget what is really important or what I need to do for the day. It makes me feel good to go shopping for clothes at one of my favourite stores or even food shopping or indulging in sweets. I'm living in that moment, enjoying it fully until I realise how much money I've spent, which leaves me with regret.

The second thing listed is the lust of the eyes. Satan tests us with our heart's desires—the temptation of taking the easy way out. In Luke 4:5-8, Satan tempted Jesus with having all the authority and glory if He worshipped him. Jesus was sent to earth to bring us eternal life through His death on the cross. Jesus knew the amount of pain He would have to go through to die for our sins, but He still refused to take the easy route.

It's very enticing to give in to this temptation when we're in a difficult situation, but it doesn't mean it's the right way or the only way. Multiple times I've wanted to run away from my children just so I can hear myself think or to simply sit in silence, to do nothing and relax. It sounds like bliss when I say it like that. It's something I truly desire; to have a break every now and then. There's nothing wrong with a break, but when I want it daily, well that's just selfish! It is literally running away from my kids and my responsibilities.

Thirdly, 1 John 2 speaks of the 'pride of life'. When we start thinking we don't need God, and we'd rather do things our own way, our faith is tested! Satan takes you to a new level of pride and then tempts you to throw your life into sin. In Luke 4:9-12, Jesus was taken to the highest point of the temple and tempted to test God. Would God save Him if He tried to kill Himself? Thankfully, Jesus stood firm, and the devil left Him. It doesn't pay to bargain or gamble with God!

Teariki and I have been through a lot of rough times, times that have tested us individually and as a couple. I must admit when things got heated, I have refused to apologise and to keep my big mouth shut. I let my pride tell me I wasn't wrong, that it was all his fault, and that I shouldn't be the one apologising. I would get myself worked up for all the wrong reasons. I knew I could've walked away to avoid an argument, but I didn't. I chose to ignore God and acted out in my disobedience—I did what I wanted to do. The problem is, that's exactly what the enemy wants! He is the destroyer of families. His aim is to keep us from living righteous, godly lives. I encourage you to be more aware of the real enemy and his tactics and strategies. When we understand how the devil tries to distract us, we can be ready to stand our ground and stay true to the calling on our lives!

25

The Enemy

For God has not given us a spirit of fear, but of power and of love and of a sound mind.

2 Timothy 1:7, NKJV

Have you ever felt something shift in your home but you can't quite put your finger on it? Maybe the kids start squabbling, or things start breaking down. Perhaps everyone feels tired all of a sudden, or anxious, or overwhelmed. There's a reason the atmosphere shifts. The enemy wants to disrupt your peace, to distract you from what God has given you to do, and to destroy the very thing you are trying to build! He actively works against us!

It happens the other way too—perhaps the mood is good, everyone's looking out for each other, and things at home tick along smoothly. That's not by accident either. Things shift when we engage in the battle through worship and prayer. I have learnt that we, as mums, can change the atmosphere in our homes, simply by partnering with God. We need to get good at spiritual warfare!

Spiritual warfare comes in many forms, but I assure you we all face it one way or another. Whether we are aware of it or not, a fight is taking place in the spiritual realm over you and me, your children, your partner, and your family. We can't have this mentality of not needing to join the battle simply because God's angels are fighting for us. It's not up to them to do all the work! No, they are fighting on your behalf, for your life, for your soul, but we need to play our part, joining the spiritual battle in prayer. Prayer is the lifeline of our spirit. Just as we need oxygen to breathe, we need prayer to keep us spiritually alive.

We also need to protect our minds. Operating from a negative mindset is very dangerous and can open the door for evil to creep in and have its way, making you vulnerable to yet more temptation. My mind is regularly being attacked. It's a constant battle and it takes a lot of discipline to shut out the negative thoughts.

The devil is a liar, and he gains ground in our lives when we agree with his lies. This is why our minds are so often attacked. Our thoughts trigger our emotions, and leads us to a reaction. The mind is very powerful, and if my thoughts aren't aligned with God's, my emotions can get overwhelming. I start to have feelings of despair, fear, and loneliness. There are many other feelings that may surface too, depending on what triggers me. And it all starts from a single thought. For example, if my mind dwells on the thought of one of my children dying, I will sometimes tear up, and soon that sadness can turn to fear. But when I declare the truth over my life, that God has destined my children for life, not death, the fear goes away and I realise that my family truly has a hope and a future.

I've also experienced Satan's attacks physically. I was heavily pregnant when I started writing this book, and out of nowhere, I get hit with flu-like symptoms, my tummy started cramping like labour pains, and suddenly I was having contractions. My whole body was in pain, especially my right arm. Surges of pain started going up and down my arm, preventing me to write. Of course, I could have just put it down to the fact I was about to give birth. But I knew there was more to what was going on. I began declaring scripture over myself and asked Teariki to lay hands on me and pray. Straight away, the cramping and pains went away!

When you begin working in your gifts, or doing the very thing God has called you to do, the enemy will hit you with difficulties, distractions and obstacles. All these tactics have one purpose—to get you out of alignment with God and throw you off track.

As a mum, I find the busyness of life often hinders me from serving God effectively. I can allow myself to become so busy with motherly duties—the laundry, cleaning the house, and food shopping. All these things are essential and need to be done but it's what I *wasn't* doing that allowed the devil in. He used these distractions and kept me busy to the point where I couldn't spend time with God and be in His Word. For many years, I allowed it to happen. It got to a point where I didn't want to read my Bible. Instead, I wanted to catch up on house chores and watch Netflix. The method Satan used was small instalments of busyness over a long period of time. He worked his way in slowly.

Thankfully, Jesus knows what we face. He told us that in this life we would experience troubles and that our battle is against the principalities of evil and not of flesh and blood. But He also said we do not need to worry. In John 16:33 (NKJV), we read: "These things I have spoken to you, that in Me you may have peace. In the world you will have tribulation; but be of good cheer, I have overcome the world."

If the enemy has gained ground in your home, it's time to rise up and join the battle for your family. We can do this confidently, knowing that the battle is already won. The great news is that we don't need to do it alone. In Christ, Satan is already defeated!

26

No Excuses

*Work with enthusiasm, as though you were
working for the Lord rather than for people.*

Ephesians 6:7, NLT

Just when I thought God was done with me, He reminded me of another assignment that was spoken over me as a young mum. He wanted me to write a book. I was overwhelmed with self-doubt. "I'm not worthy to write a book," and "I don't know big, sophisticated words," rushed through my mind. I was scared of the opinions I would receive but having learnt from my earlier experiences, I stopped complaining and got started. I now know that when we're working in the assignment that God sets before us, we get to truly find out what our purpose is.

Writing this book has been a journey. In the time it's taken me to complete it, so much has happened. I don't think I've ever endured trials quite like what I faced and overcame during this process. With six children to care for and Teariki working away from home, the only way this book was going to get written was by persevering late into the night, going without sleep and pressing into God even when I was beyond exhausted, working on no sleep. I had to determine to do the incredible thing God had placed in my spirit. I can testify that my walk with God has been shaken and flipped upside down to the point where I can't keep using the same old excuses to procrastinate!

As a parent, I often use my children as an excuse to get out of things. It's either that they're sick or I have no babysitter, or I'm too tired because my baby kept me up all night. Even so, finding time to do what God places on my heart is always a challenge. The chores are non-stop in my house! But I've had to learn to continue in obedience. There are days where I'm waiting on God to move me when really, God is waiting on me! He wants me to move forward and become who He has created me to be. He wants me to step into my purpose. There is a reason why I am here today. It's not only to be the mother to my children or write a book—it's also to go out into this world and share the goodness of God with others. I'm not going to lie, it is not the easiest task, and it can be scary. The fear of other people's opinions and not knowing how they could react can hinder my willingness to step out and share about God's love.

I've learnt that if God has something for you to do or wants you to go somewhere it is actually a privilege. I go so that others can receive a blessing as well. When I choose to step out in faith and obedience, I'm putting the needs of others before my own and someone else gets blessed. Think about that for a bit. I don't want anyone to miss out on the blessings of what God has for them because I failed to obey and chose to give into fear. It's not about me, it's about others. Being a mother and a parent, you are already putting the needs of your children before your own, so there is no need for excuses in any other area of life! People often ask me how I manage six children while my partner is away working yet still find the time to attend church, followship with others, and maintain myself. The answer is simple: It's not me, it's all God.

Without a doubt, the only way I can do all that I do is because I have confidence in God. God-confidence means depending completely on God and His strength to handle the things in your life.

Now all I need to learn is to use this God-confidence and share it with others. Everyone in this world is engaged in a fight with their own brokenness. Everyone is battling against sin and the enemy's schemes so often disguised as financial stress, relationship troubles, addiction, depression and suicide. We all need a dose of God's love!

I have been chosen by God and given a specific skill that He wants me to use. He wants me to be successful at it, not as the world sees success, but simply the success of completing the work I am given to do. God does not make mistakes in who He chooses. He chooses wisely for the task at hand, but I still need to be disciplined. I need to walk in righteousness and with integrity before I start to move in His greatness. I still have a lot of work to do on myself, but I've decided to do the work and invest time with God to make sure I stay on the right path.

I have to live one day at a time, placing one foot in front of the other, and be ready to move when He tells me to—it's called walking by faith. When I'm trying to walk in His will, it's never easy, but the Lord always slides something solid under me to cushion the landing. I'm still growing in this, trying to stand on His Word and learning how to apply His Word despite my feelings. "No more excuses" looks like moving past my fear, trusting the Word of the Lord, and believing that no matter what you are dealing with, God is with us! I offer you these words of encouragement: It is time! No more excuses!

You are chosen.

    You are enough.

        You are worthy.

            And you are qualified.

In Closing

As a little girl, if you were to ask me what I wanted to be, I would have said, "I have no idea." I never would've thought I would be where I am today. I remember as a teenager saying to my friends that I didn't want to have children. I saw my mother and the challenges she faced, and I never wanted that for myself. I saw having children as a barrier to freedom. But isn't it funny how God works? The very thing you don't want, or don't expect to do or have, He comes along and says that's the very thing He's going to bless you with. And for me, He did exactly that.

Now, I am a mother of six children, ranging in age from thirteen to a three-month-old baby. My little family is overrun by females. Sometimes I pity my partner and my two sons! Can you imagine yourself surrounded by little girls who all reflect different traits of you, plus carrying their own little 'challenging' traits? I experience that on a daily basis. My girls all have different personalities, and let me tell you, it is hard trying to interact with all of them! But thank God, He gives me everything I need to succeed at this—not bad for someone who never wanted any children!

The thing is, I cannot imagine how my life would have gone if Jesus had not been part of it. I can admit now that God used my children to save

IN CLOSING

me from a life of alcoholism, drugs, and living a fake life surrounded by fake people. Motherhood forced me to become more mature. I had little human beings that I had to take care of, and although I felt like a total failure and believed I was a total screw up, I now know that is not true, thank God! God accepted me how I was at the time—a single mother with an abusive past who felt inadequate and unworthy. I'm glad to say now that was me then, but this is me now . . . a mother, a woman, and a precious child of the King.

God knows I have so much more to offer. I often fall back into self-doubt, thinking I'm not enough and I have nothing left to offer. Being a mother is the most difficult thing a woman can be. I know I'm not the only one who finds it hard! Every day has challenges of its own, many of them to do with my children. I try every day to walk in righteousness and be a light for Christ to my children. We will never fully understand the reason why some things happen in our lives and every day I fear for my children. It's a normal human emotion, but it's what we do with that fear that makes the difference. When I fail, or when fear pops up in my heart, I always give it to God. I use it as a reminder to be thankful that my blessings are alive and breathing, and in good health. I now savour when they say, "I love you, Mum." The fears I face as a mother are what push me towards God and cause me to lean solely on Him.

I've experienced living a worldly life and it's not for me. My experiences of the world are the reason why I choose to be planted in a church and have a personal relationship with Jesus. It is my greatest hope to see my children live the life God intended them to live. I'm a normal, everyday person, with much to learn about being a woman, and a mother. I'm not perfect, that's for certain. Regardless of how many children I have, I do not have all the answers. But I do have hope for my family's future.

Jeremiah 29:11 (NLT) says: "For I know the plans I have for you," says the Lord. "They are plans for good and not for disaster, to give you a future and a hope."

When you're unsure of what to do next or if you feel stuck, remember this promise. It has given me hope in circumstances where most people would give up. Without fail, our heavenly Father has shown me a way out, and He can for you too.

This is me—and this is my testimony of how Jesus saved me, not once but multiple times and I know there will be more to come. He has everything planned out for me. All I have to do is follow Him and let Him guide me. And that is true for you too. In God's strength, you have got this, Mama!

www.ingramcontent.com/pod-product-compliance
Lightning Source LLC
Chambersburg PA
CBHW031257290426
44109CB00012B/629